LOSS AND GRIEF

Caitie McAneney

New York

Published in 2015 by The Rosen Publishing Group, Inc.
29 East 21st Street, New York, NY 10010

First Edition

Editor: Caitie McAneney
Book Design: Mickey Harmon

Photo Credits: Cover (series logo) Alhovik/Shutterstock.com; cover (banner) moham'ed/Shutterstock.com; (father and son) Peter Cade/The Image Bank/Getty Images; back cover, pp. 3, 4, 6, 8, 10, 12, 14, 15, 16, 18, 20, 22–24 (background) Matyas Szabo/Shutterstock.com; p. 5 Image Point Fr/Shutterstock.com; p. 7 RubberBall Productions/Vetta/Getty Images; p. 9 Rob Marmion/Shutterstock.com; p. 10 Olimpik/Shutterstock.com; p. 11 Tom Wang/Shutterstock.com; p. 13 Anton Watman/Shutterstock.com; p. 14 Jacek Chabraszewski/Shutterstock.com; p. 15 Kathleen Finlay/Cultura/Getty Images; p. 17 Gladskikh Tatiana/Shutterstock.com; p. 19 wavebreakmedia/Shutterstock.com; p. 21 Suzanne Tucker/Shutterstock.com; p. 22 gemphoto/Shutterstock.com.

Library of Congress Cataloging-in-Publication Data

McAneney, Caitlin.
  Loss and grief / Caitie McAneney.
    pages cm. — (Let's talk about it)
  Includes index.
  ISBN 978-1-4777-5791-8 (pbk.)
  ISBN 978-1-4777-5796-3 (6 pack)
  ISBN 978-1-4777-5798-7 (library binding)
  1. Loss (Psychology) 2. Death. 3. Grief. I. Title.
  BF575.D35M348 2015
  152.4—dc23
                            2014024181

Manufactured in the United States of America

CPSIA Compliance Information: Batch #CW15PK: For Further Information contact Rosen Publishing, New York, New York at 1-800-237-9932

CONTENTS

BAD NEWS

At some point, everyone goes through a loss. A loss might leave you feeling **confused**, hurt, sad, or even angry. It could bring about an unwanted change in your life.

There are different kinds of loss. You might have to move, which means your home life will change. Your parents might be getting a divorce, which means your family life will change. One of the worst kinds of loss is when someone close to you dies. You may feel that life will never be the same again.

When you first hear bad news, it might be hard to fully understand it. It's normal to feel that the news isn't "real" yet.

WHAT IS GRIEF?

Grief is the way a person **reacts** to loss. There are many different grief reactions. You might feel pain in your body, such as a stomachache. You might have trouble paying attention or sleeping. You could find yourself thinking often about the person who died. You might feel strong **emotions**.

Grieving may feel painful, but it's a normal and healthy way to deal with loss. At first, the **challenge** might be understanding the death. Then, the challenge will be learning to live without your loved one.

Many people go to **funerals** when someone dies. This is one way to say goodbye, which is a part of their grieving.

TELL ME MORE

Everyone has a different way of grieving. Some people might be angry, and some might be sad. Some people might want to talk about it, and others might not.

7

UNDERSTANDING

You may have a lot of questions after you lose someone. Some questions might be answered easily. What happened? How did it happen? You can ask a family member, such as a parent, to explain it to you. Maybe your loved one was very sick or old. Maybe they died because of an awful event, such as a car crash.

You may have harder questions. Why did this happen? What happens to someone after death? Adults may be able to share what they believe with you.

It can be hard to understand death, especially when it happens quickly or to someone who was young. Your parents might be confused, too. Finding some answers can help you feel better.

It may be hard to hear the truth about how your loved one died. It's okay if you're not ready to have answers yet.

9

FEELINGS

It's normal to have many bad feelings after someone dies, such as sadness, loneliness, anger, and fear. You'll probably be sad because you'll miss your loved one. You might feel lonely because they're not around. Adults might look upset, too. They're going through their own grief.

TELL ME MORE

You might not feel anything at first because you're in shock. That's normal, too.

The first step to feeling better is to accept your feelings. Let yourself feel sad or angry. If you feel like crying, let yourself cry. This is part of grieving. Letting your emotions out helps you to heal.

Bad feelings usually go away after enough time if you accept them.

WHY ANGER?

Sometimes people feel angry after loss. If someone you love dies in an accident, you might be angry with the person who caused it. If someone dies of an illness, you might be angry with the doctors who couldn't save them.

You might be angry with the person who died because it seems like they left you. It's even normal to be angry with yourself. Maybe you feel that you could have done something to save the person who died. But placing blame only causes more hurt.

TELL ME MORE

It's okay to be angry. It probably feels unfair that this is happening to you and your family. It helps to share your feelings with an adult.

If you're angry with yourself, remember that it's not your fault and that you cannot change what has already happened.

FEELING SCARED

It's normal to feel scared after someone dies. Losing someone is a big change in your life. It can make you feel uneasy about everything else. You might be scared that other loved ones will die. Maybe you find yourself trying to be around your parents all the time.

TELL ME MORE

If you see your parents crying, you might be afraid they can't take care of you anymore. But they're just grieving, and soon they'll be better, too.

You might be afraid that something bad will happen to you. Maybe you don't feel as safe anymore. For example, if your friend dies of cancer, you might be afraid you'll get cancer, too.

It's important to tell your fears to an adult. They'll be able to explain why you shouldn't be worried. For example, your dad can tell you that you can't catch cancer from others.

TALKING IT OUT

The best thing to do when you're grieving is talk to someone about it. A parent might answer your questions or tell you what usually makes them feel better. A friend, brother, or sister can talk to you, too. They can listen and maybe give **advice**. Maybe they're feeling the same things. This can bring your family and friends closer together.

You can also write your feelings in a journal. Write about what happened, what your loved one meant to you, and how you feel about it.

It can help you to help others feel better. Ask your family and friends how they feel about losing their loved one. You can help each other to grieve.

TELL ME MORE

There are many ways to let your feelings out. You can even draw pictures in your journal that show your feelings.

KEEPING MEMORIES ALIVE

When you lose someone, it might make you feel better to think of your happy memories of them. Think about what made that person special. Was she a great cook? Did he sing in the car? Think of these things when you're feeling sad.

You will still miss the person who died. You'll never have them back completely. But you can gather pictures of the person to look at when you miss them. You can remember the good things they used to do and say.

Getting over your grief doesn't mean forgetting about your loved one. You can keep their memory alive, even when you start to feel better.

DEALING WITH CHANGE

After someone dies, it might be hard to live your everyday life in the same way. It may be hard to pay attention in school. You might not enjoy your hobbies anymore. Maybe you feel **guilty** about having fun when your loved one is gone.

It's important to keep living your **routine**. Going to school, practicing a sport or hobby, and playing with friends can help you to feel like some things are still normal. Routines can help you **adjust** to life after your loved one's death.

> Certain things will be different. Maybe holiday dinners will seem different without your loved one. But it's important to keep making new memories with your family and friends.

If you find it very hard to pay attention in school or do your everyday activities, tell a parent or teacher so they can help you.

21

BETTER IN TIME

How long does grieving take? Some people might feel better after only a few weeks. It could take months or years to feel okay about the death of a loved one. Sometimes bad feelings come in waves. One minute you'll feel fine, and the next you're sad again.

Be **patient** with yourself as you grieve. Just like when you break a bone, it can take a while to heal. Live one day at a time, and some day soon, you'll start feeling better.

GLOSSARY

adjust: To change to fit new conditions.

advice: An opinion about how to handle a problem.

challenge: A thing that is hard to deal with.

confused: Unable to understand something.

emotion: A strong feeling.

funeral: The service held when burying the dead.

guilty: Feeling that you have done something wrong.

patient: Waiting calmly for something.

react: To act because something has happened.

routine: A regular course of action.

INDEX

A
afraid, 14, 15
angry, 4, 7, 10, 11, 12, 13
answers, 8, 9, 16

C
confused, 4, 8

E
emotions, 6, 11

F
fear, 10, 15
feelings, 10, 11, 12, 14, 16, 17, 18, 22
funerals, 7

G
guilty, 20

H
happy memories, 18

J
journal, 16, 17

P
pain, 6

Q
questions, 8, 16

R
reactions, 6
routines, 20

S
sad, 4, 7, 10, 11, 18, 22

T
talk, 7, 16
trouble paying attention, 6, 20, 21

WEBSITES

Due to the changing nature of Internet links, PowerKids Press has developed an online list of websites related to the subject of this book. This site is updated regularly. Please use this link to access the list: www.powerkidslinks.com/ltai/loss